Poems for Life

Kimberly Capracotta

Presentation by *BookLeaf Publishing*

Web: www.bookleafpub.com

E-mail: info@bookleafpub.com

ISBN: 9789358310535

First edition 2023

Love

Love comes
Soundless
Into our hearts.

Love comes
Blazingly
Into our lives.

Love comes
Singing
Joy and happiness.

Love comes
Brandishing
Swords of pain.

Love comes
In the
Darkness.

Love comes
In the
Light.

Love comes

And
Love hides.

Love comes
To stay
Forever.

Love comes
To say
Goodbye.

Love comes
To breathe
New life.

Love comes
And cannot
Destroy.

Love comes
In many
Shapes.

Love comes
In many
Ways.

Love makes
Life

Tricky.

Love is
Not
Predictable.

Most of all
Always know

Love comes
For you.

The Rose

In the middle of the forest
In the deep dark wood
Grows a single rose
That is misunderstood.

How much is legend,
How much is true -
People have been seeking
The answer generations through.

Glories and riches,
Fame and power,
Are all to come
To the one with the flower.

On a dark cold night,
Two wizards seek
To find the rose
And no longer be weak.

Like many others
They just don't understand
What it means
To take the rose in hand.

Searching for glory
The two battle this winter
Desperately wanting
The rose in the center.

Many seek
But few are chosen
To learn true power comes
When love is unfrozen.

You see the rose
Is the one to impart
That glory and power
Can only come from the heart.

Prayer at the Beach

Dear Lord,

I can't hear you right now,
The noise in my head
As loud as this surf.

But I believe you see me.
I believe you hear me.
I believe you know me.

I hate how I feel.

I hate that I have trouble seeing
All of your creation as beautiful.

You know each one of these people.
You know their minds and hearts.
You see them as you see me.

But all I see right now is frightening.
Every single one seems a potential threat,
From the old lady to the tiny baby.

I don't like what society is doing.
But I don't know how to affect it.
I want to make things better if I could.

I don't believe You sent this.
I don't believe it is a punishment.
You already took care of that for us.

I do believe only You can help me
To make it through.
Only You know how I can live.

I miss living.
I miss laughing.
I want more than survival.

You already know what I want -
For the world, for others,

And for myself.

I have no idea
If anything I want
Is what You want.

I don't know if prayer matters.
I don't understand if praying for something
Really gets us anything.

I don't know a lot of things,
But I want to know everything
Deeper.

Am I ungrateful?
I know I worry more than I should
And don't outwardly appreciate what I have.

I am not ungrateful.
I know I am highly privleged
And have anything I physically need.

I just don't have what I want.
And have things I don't want.
And my mind has trouble.

I am a seeker, a questioner,
A worrier and a giver and a fixer.
You know because you know me.

You gave me a mind that can see
Big and small, good, bad…
But something has gone glitchy.

I see too much negative.
Or I can see positive but negative focuses.
I just want to fix everything.

But I can't.
I don't know how to give or help others right
now
Because I can't fix my own mind.

You made me beautifully,
The world beat me up once before.
You started putting me back together.

But now I wonder if I have tarnished me.
Have I tried to destroy the beauty again?
Why?

How do You see me?
The same as every one of these people?
Am I as beautiful to you as the day you made
me?

I don't feel it right now.
I can see the good stuff I still do.

But I am not feeling it.

I am lonely.
It has been a long time
Since I felt loneliness like this.

The world went away,
I wasn't prepared.
I don't understand how others are.

I don't want to feel like this.
I don't want to be like this.
I don't want the world to hurt, too.

I want to laugh again.
I want to be held
I want to feel wanted.

I want to be comfort
And be comforted.
I want to help.

But I just don't know how.
So I ask because maybe I haven't before -
Will you please help me?

Spirit

Back and forth.
Faster, slower.
Stalks bend
But do not break.
Air.
Moving gently,
Moving fast,
Moving. Moving.
Element for life.
Potential destruction.
Waves flow
Always existing
Never ending
Back and forth.
Faster, slower.

Little Star

She always yearned to be
Among the nighttime stars.
Their glow so appealing,
Enchanting beauty.
Yet destiny seemed to have her
Grounded to the earth below.
She could not climb
Could not fly
To be the light

In the universe.

It came to pass
That the nights grew darker
As did the days.
She still looked
But the stars grew dim
Until she could see them no more.

The world was dark and cold
And she could not find the light.

And then she saw it.
On a cold night,
A light soared through the sky.

She wished for a way back.
She wished to bring back the light.

The moon was nearby
And saw her darkness.
He did not like to see her so sad.

One night the moon came to her.
He said, Come dance with me.

But you are so far away,
She told him,
I cannot get to you

I do not know how.

Have faith,
Take the path that is lit before you.

She knew she had a choice.
She could remain
And stay in the dark tunnels
Of the earth.

Or she could follow
This dimly illuminated path
Into a world of mystery.

She stepped forward.
The path seemed to end.
Come on,
Said the moon.

She jumped.

And the moon was there for her,
Catching her in
A dazzle of light.

The moon showed her
Many wonders
Among the stars.

She found a light
For herself
That started coming from
Inside.

With the moon,
She finally felt safe
And loved.
No one was going to hurt her.

She danced in the heavens,
Her smile a comet
Sailing by.
Her laugh a shimmer
Twirling around her.

And then the moon told her,
I have to leave you
For a little while.

No, no, no,
She can't lose it all.
She just found this light.
She just found this joy.

My darling, the moon said,
I am not your source of light.
My light is only a reflection.
But you —

You always had the light within.
You are my light,
My joy,
And my sunshine.

And though it may seem
Dark for a while,
I will be back
And we will dance
Through the stars
Together again.

Keep shining bright,
So we can be again.

And so she waited.
And she tried hard to keep
Burning bright.

Light flares with her temper,
Light dims with her gloom.
But always light she keeps
For her moon.

Sit with Me

Come and sit with me.
Let me see the sky
In your eyes.

Come and sit with me.
Feel my lips
On yours.

Come and sit with me.
Let us speak
Of truth.

Come and sit with me.

Wrap me in your arms
To be part of you.

Come and sit with me.
Please
Don't let me go.

We

If I am me
And you are you,
I ask
Who are we?

Am I the milk
And you the honey
To sweeten the jokes
That make life funny?

Are you the sun
And I the moon
Who make the
Lovers swoon?

Am I the secret
And you the truth
Wrapped together,
Stealing youth?

Do you fly
While I crawl;
Angel and devil
Sees us all?

For our sake
Must we be
Opposite the other
For eternity?

Can we enhance
Each other's life,
As we come together
And swallow pride?

Give me some of your light,
I will give you some dark,
Then together
We balance our hearts.

Let this question
Forever be ours
In the dark of night

Find our light.

If I am me
And you are you
Then my darling
Who are we?

Harmony

She hears something
Tapping faintly
In the distance.

Tap-
Tap-
Tap-

She tilts her head,
Tracking the sound,
And turns to face the earth.

Tap-
Tap-
Tap-

A lone figure
Dancing
Along the sea shore.

Tap-
Tap-
Tap-

The emotions radiated
A swirl of colors
Twisting a ribbon rainbow.

Tap-
Tap-
Tap-

She watches him;
Drawn by a rhythm
Resonating in her heart.

-tatap
-tatap
-tatap

Something feels
As if it touches his heart;
He pauses.

-tatap
-tatap
-tatap

Again the ripple,
He feels it,
Gliding alongside his aura.

-tatap
-tatap
-tatap

He turns and looks to the stars,
That bright star,
He never noticed it before.

-tatap
-tatap
-tatap

The starlight seems to reach
Toward him,
Enveloping him.

-tatap
-Tap
-tatap

He stretches,

The light takes shape,
And they come face to face.

Tap-
-tatap
Tap-
-tatap
Tap-
-tatap

Energy circles around them
Blending and binding,
Holding them together.

Tap-tatap
Tap
-tatap
Taptatap.

Each beat brings them closer,
Each sound another connection,
Holding.

Tap-tatatatap
TapTaptatap
Taptatap.

Both find joy
Both find pleasure.

Both find hope.

Taptatap
Taptatap
Taptatap

The dance takes new shape
The songs, new sounds
The lives, harmony.

I Looked Into Your Eyes

I looked into your eyes
And was amazed to see
All of you
Looking back at me.

I saw your walls
Built so high
With a tiny door
Very few can spy.

I tried to peek
And see what is hidden,
And to my amazement,
"Enter" I was bidden.

With care and love
I walked inside,
And saw a great world,
All behind your eyes.

I saw your heart,
Your loves and passions,
Sparks of joy
And flames of action.

I saw your troubles,
And the lessons they taught;
I saw your worries -
How I wish they were naught!

I could feel the fear
Of the future unknown -
I saw the dark fields,
Withering away, alone.

I heard the laughs,
The jokes and the clinks
Of the shared times
With meals and drinks!

I saw your strength,
Clad in knight's armor,
Beaten and worn
But sword made sharper.

A beautiful woman
I saw inside
A friend for life
I have come to realize.

I wanted to tell you,
I wanted to say,
Please don't be afraid,
I am with you all the way.

You can put down the sword,
You can drop the shield,
You are safe with me,
Your secrets I will not yield.

When I looked in your eyes,
I saw my friend,
All you are
And all you have been.

It does not matter
What life deals you,
Please just remember
I am always here for you -

Just look in my eyes
And we will know
A friendship that withstands

Heaven and Hell to grow.

Good, bad and all in-between,
Being with you I realize
Just what you mean -
When I look in your eyes.

For You

Like a golden thread,
You wove your way
Into my heart and soul.

You took my pain
And shared it
Just to lighten the load.

You are forever
A part of me.

You healed with
Friendship
With laughter
With love.

You let me in
Your heart
And soul

Two minds
Find harmony.
Two souls
Find peace.
Two hearts
Find love.

One day we will part
But always know
You are forever
My heart.

Mirrors

Look in the mirror.
Just randomly
See yourself
And see what lies inside.

So I look.
And I see
Things inside
Things that scare me.

Crumbled masks
Stare back
Blank eyes and cracked cheeks
Old holding on.

Beyond the empty eyes,

A tiny light,
A fire,
Over a path of choices.

The Shadow Man
Stands at the crux.
He beckons me,
But he cannot touch me yet.

His path is straight,
Easy,
Safe
He indicates.

I look away.

The other is
A winding jungle
A roaring sea
An unpredictable adventure.

I turn back to the masks.
Through the empty eyes
I can see all the me's
I used to be.

Such a good girl,
So smart and kind,
Puts others first,

Adults praise.

Internal struggles
Questions no one can
-or wants to-
Answer.

There is the rebellion.
Must not let it loose.
Conform because
You do not want to be the outcast.

The conformist
Predictable
Others feel loved
But it is not enough.

It must be enough
They tell me
It is worth it
So I trust them.

The Shadow Man appears.
He can never touch
I must go to him
But someone stops me.

Watch -
She tells me.

Where did she come from?
What does she see in me?

She is a friend,
Who can see beyond,
Who can see inside,
Who can walk with me.

I look at the masks again.
Beyond the flame,
Beyond the Shadow,
Beyond.

There is a woman,
Shackles on her wrists,
Chains broken,
Yet not quite free.

Sword beside her,
Kneels on the ground -
Head bowed
She sighs.

To be the protector
Becomes a burden,
Which she will bear
Forever.

The friend comes.

Says to the warrior -
Here,
I am here.

Take my hand,
I lend you my strength.
I cannot free you,
But I will tell you what I see.

A woman -
Oppressed and confined,
With a spirit strong
As lightning in the night.

A woman -
Fierce and brave,
Heart of the dragon,
Breathing fire upon enemies.

A woman -
Wise beyond,
Ancients and philosophers
Form her thoughts.

A woman -
Scared and afraid
For the world is not
To be changed.

A woman -
Who still hopes
Even as she wanders
And is taunted in the darkness.

A woman -
Who can love,
Is worthy of love,
And deserves it.

A woman -
Who is a friend,
A lover,
A warrior and protector.

Now warrior
Tell me
what will you choose?

Repair the masks of old,
Return to your chains,
And deny your life?

Will you run into the darkness?
Sleep deep in its arms?

Or will you rise again,
Find your fire,
Banish the shadows,

And find your fulfillment?

Look in the mirror
And see what is inside.

I Watch the Lights

I watch the lights.

Each one glides
Across the rough surfaces.

Tall and short,
Round and straight.

They look the same.
They look different.

The small ones
Shine brighter.

The tall ones
Shine harder.

Blackness enters
From below.

Light and dark
Battle inside.

Black into light
Light into black.

Some have the dark
In a little ball.

Some have the light
Almost extinguished.

Most are constantly
Rebalancing.

Swirling dark
Swirling light.

Each one glides
Across the rough surfaces.

Scars

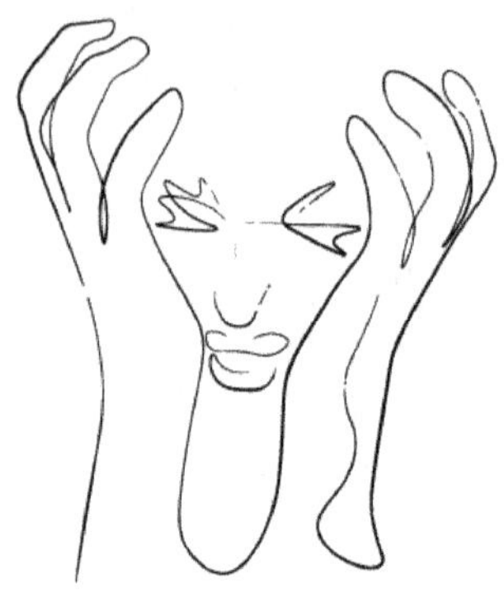

What do you see
When you look in
The reflecting glass?

Do you see
The reminders of
Struggle and pain?

The scars in the mirror,
On your body
In your mind?

Your scars are not blemishes;
They are enhancements
That show you live.

Your scars are not fences;
They are obstacles
That you have overcome.

Your scars are not shame;
They are proof
That you survive.

Your scars are not weakness;
They are evidence
That you are strong.

Your scars do not define you.
You define your scars
And show the world

Your scars did not make you
You made your scars
As you dare to live

In the world
Defying darkness,
Seeking joy.

Waves

Can't you hear the waves
Pounding on the shore?

All else is dark.
All else is silent.

Can't you hear the waves
Crashing on the land?

No birds.
No songs.

Can't you hear the waves
Pulsing against the sand?

Where is the day;
Wherefore this dark night?

I hear the waves
Pummeling at my door.

Dark water.
Dark sky.

I hear the waves
Battering my heart.

The sails are furled,
Boats run aground.

I hear the waves,
Shadows in the storm.

Cuts and scrapes,
Soaked and scarred.

I hear the waves,
Taking me down.

Fight the drowning,
Hold on tight.

I hear the waves,

Coming more and more.

Day breaks,
Sending away terror of the night.

Can you hear the waves
Retreating from the shore?

Light returns,
Darkness fades.

Can you hear the waves?
I can no more.

Companion

I walked in the crowd
Alone among the many;
People pass, I give a small smile -
People pass, never seeing.

I am met by another,
She resembles me,
But is covered
With scars and bruises.

She does not speak,
But falls in step,
I say Hello
But she just walks with me.

My new companion and I -
Oddly quiet
But a familiarity
Exists between us -

We walk farther along,
The crowds begin
To blur in my sight
As my eyes narrow

On the path ahead.
Another steps out,
Dressed in purple-black
And proceeds to speak -

"Fate has dealt her lethal hand
Yours to look at, to play -
Is it worthy? Is it fair?
Fate has given you your destiny.

" Robbed of joy,
Friendship a lie,
Happiness taken
This is your life - you must die."

My quiet companion,
Fair skin turns bright,
More markings appear
Yet she is ready to fight -

"Bitterness - you jealous thing-
You know nothing of this world you sing.
Fate may deal but she does not play,
Only the living have the final say

In how the world will see
What is obvious to you and me -
She will choose her path to follow,
And you will be left behind in the hollow."

With that speech, Bitteness did shrink -
I saw behind her mask of disgust,
My own face distorted and fade away,
As she became small and walked with us.

I turned to my Companion,
I saw her freshly again,
Scars torn open, she breathes heavily,
I speak to her with a puzzled look -

"What is this -
This thing we are doing?
Who are you and who is she?
Why are you all following me?"

My Companion looked at me
A soft light in her eyes.
She gently shakes her head
And then I began to see…

An otherworldly shriek
Pierced the crowd
And like a lightning bolt
Another was in our space.

This girl, a distortion of me,
Set upon us
Fierce as a dragon

To deliver her own truth -

"Anger is one of my many names,
I come to poke and prod
And bring you hate
That you may see the world

"And understand it is too late.
You cannot save it,
nothing more can be done,
All is lost in the war."

My Companion again
Grows mighty,
She glows with light
And speaks to Anger -

"You are a shadow,
A childish emotion -
A tantrum -
A sick little notion.

You may exist as a balance,
But you will not rule,
This one's life,
For she will choose what is just and right."

And with those words,
Anger did shrink,

And head facing down,
Walked beside Bitterness.

Once again I looked at my Companion
She looked tired and weak,
Yet her complexion was changing,
Pink now in her cheeks.

I began to implore
And then thought again,
It was not yet time
To discover the identity of my new friend.

We walked along, the four of us,
Then came the biggest of demons
From the darkest shadows
Bellowing in his approach -

"You are not enough,
You know this is true,
For if you were,
Why did your friends reject you?

You are responsible
For all that has happened-
You needed to much,
You pushed them away,

You do not understand

How to be what they want
You cannot be who you think you are
Because that is just a fantasy

A wish in a star!
In all the centuries I have lived,
There has never been any like you
And that is what they all said."

I looked to my Companion,
Expecting her to rise again,
But instead she looked at me,
And spoke,

"This demon is yours alone,
Only you can bring him down,
It is time for you to make your choice -
Tell us - will Fate be your clown?"

I studied my Companion's face,
Like in a mirror,
In her eyes I saw my strength -
My weapon of choice - my Hope.

I faced the newest presence,
Spoke calmly and said -
"I know who you are
And you speak Truth -

"There has never been any like me -
And that is certain,
I am one in a million,
And you have come

"To try to break me down once more?
No, no,
Never again -
Never will I believe your many lies

"You live in my head,
You Dark King
You take Self-Doubt -
 make her your queen.

"Bitterness and Anger
Are your daughters,
Grief and Jealousy
Your sons -

"And in your kingdom,
Who is the Fool,
Who the Jester?
Do you think it me?

"It is upon your head,
You wear the three-belled crown,
Motley colors
Of sickly red and brown.

"Fool-King of Darkness,
I know you well,
You are Depression,
A liar and hell-l hound .

"You darken my path
On days I am happy,
You send raging storms
When I am sad.

"But I have the one thing
That can defeat you,
Keep you at bay -
She is here with me today.

"My Companion,
So abused yet sweet,
She shields me, gains scars and bruises,
And yet the abuse is from my own hand.

"Here I finally see,
My Companion lies
Within my soul,
She is my shield and my sword.

"Her name is Hope
And she is strong,
Her inner light always burning,

Burning out of love.

"She has been hurt and beaten,
But yet she survives,
She rises from the ashes,
A Phoenix of gold,

"A beauty inside -
Inside me is where she dwells,
It is in fighting you and your demons,
I feel her swell.

"You see, Dark King,
You twist truths and outright lie,
And I sometimes believe you -
But in the end, there is only one

"On whom I can rely -
Not you, not at all
But on my Companion-
Who is really - Me."

With that final understanding,
A chain appeared in my hand,
I bound the Dark King and
Secured him.

"I will not banish you -
I know it isn't that simple,

But I will say you will not rule
My heart again.

"I am greater than you
And your lies -
I have faith in those who love me,
And hope in humankind.

"But most of all,
I know myself."

The Dark King became small,
Small as his demon daughters,
And fell in line,
Walking in shame behind me.

I looked upon my Companion once more,
And I notice she was glowing,
A halo of light and warmth surround her
And she spoke -

"You know who I am,
I am always your Companion.
I am Hope, springing forth from Love,
For the betterment of the world.

"You know who you are,
You are my Companion, my hands, my body-
Let me see the world, the potential,

And be the Hope and Love for those you meet."

With that, she disappeared,
Yet I felt lighter inside.
My demons still followed me,
But I know how to tame them.

Now I walk through the crowds once more,
Seeing the people as they pass,
A genuine smile, a kind word -
Yes, I know who I am

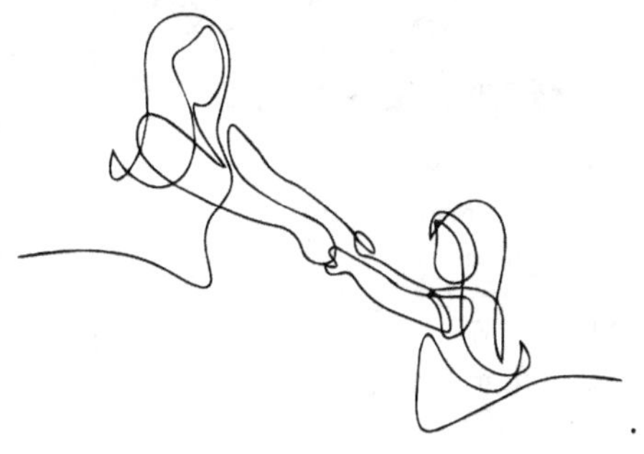

Every Day is Hard

Everyday is so hard.
The world has gone mad.

People are crazy,
Even more than normal.

We are given so many different
Rules and recommendations.

How do we know what to do
Everyday?

Wash your hands,
That should be for always.

Don't invade personal space.
That would prevent a lot of problems.

Don't talk, look, or breathe.
This is a problem.

Everyday is so hard.
I miss you.

A Year

1 year.
52 weeks.
365 days.
525,600 minutes.

The last shared smiles,
The last shared touch,
The last shared secrets.

My world collapsed,
My heart fell,
I was afraid.

You were gone,
We both worried,
I couldn't help you.

We made our choices,
We continued on,
As we could.

After all this time,
My heart is different,
My world is forever changed.

But I know more
About love
And you and me.

Everything we shared,
Everything we cared,
Everything is still there.

Even now,
Even after
One year.

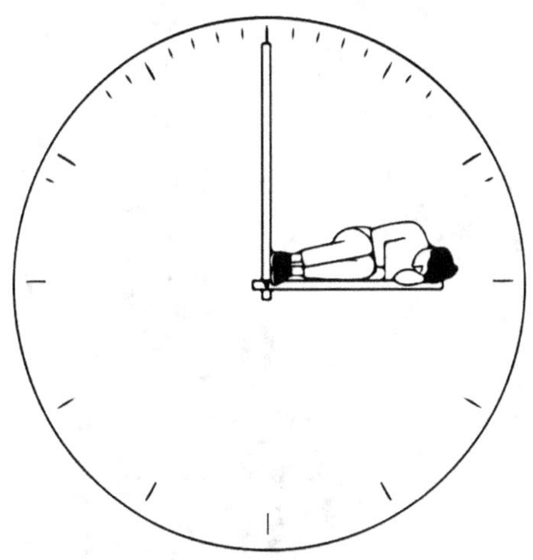

Anticipation

Anticipation.
She has been waiting for so long.
Nervous excitement.
What to wear?
What will please him?
Be pretty.
Be nice.
Smile.
Be beautiful.
Will he even care?
Why wouldn't he?

Weeks since she saw him.
Heard him.
Touched him.
Butterflies inside her.
She has to pee for the hundreth time -
Dang nervous bladder.

Excitement.
Fear.
Rolled into one.
She waits.
Where is he?
She is early.
She is trembling.

Don't let him see it.
Control your emotions.

Breathe - breathe - breathe.

Think about the good.
His jokes.
His mind.
His taste.
His body.
Hands on her.
Everywhere.
Pulls her close.
His kiss.

But -

What if he does not want her?
The panic, the tears, the pain.

Don't let him see it.
Control your emotions.
Breathe; breathe; breathe.

Oh! but what if he does?
What if he still wants
Her cute butt.
Her smile.
Her beauty.
Her depth.

Trembling.
Shaking.
Anticipation.
Nervous excitement.

Don't let him see it.
Control your emotions.
Breathe, breathe, breathe.

So many weeks.
Days.
Hours.
Is it really almost time?

Don't cry.
Don't be mean.
Don't babble.

Don't let him see....
Control your emotions.
Breathe breathe breathe.

Whatif-whatif-whatif.
Her mind races.
So many possible reactions.
One opportunity.
She tries to prepare.
She cannot.
Excitement and fear

Entwined.

She waits.
The clock stills
But her heart flies.

That's him.
He's here.
Oh God.
So many feelings.

Don't let him see.
Control your emotions.
BreatheBreatheBreathe.

Don't cry.

Don't .

Cry.

What will he do?
She missed him.
Wants him.
Did he miss her?
Want her?

Don't cry, don't cry, don't cry.

The shaking inside does not stop.
Is it just inside?

Don't let him see.
Control.
Breathe.

Her question will soon be answered.
Body quivering.
Heart pounding.
Mind racing.

He smiles.
She calms.
"Hi," he says.
"Hi," she says.

Let him see.
Do not control.
Breathe.
Breathe.
Breathe.

He comes toward her.
Anticpation.
Nervous excitement.
Butterflies.
Waiting.

And she has her answer.

Heartshare

How does one heart
Hold so much?

How can I feel
Confusion and confidence?

Why is there both
Love and pain?

In a single instance,
Darkness and light -

How does one heart
Hold so much?

Who holds the key
To balance the dichotomy -

That exists
Within me?

Is there another
Or only You

To steady my heartbeat
And show me the Way?

How does one heart
Hold so much?

I look and look
And seek to find

A light for my darkness,
A hope to shine -

To find a Truth
In this conflicting world.

Where, O where -

Please speak and say!

How does one heart
Hold so much?

I am told there is comfort,
I am told there is peace,

If rules are followed,
I can be free.

I struggle and try,
And fail everyday

To be the good girl they say
You want me to be.

How does one heart
Hold so much?

Failure and guilt
Eternal shame

Have been taught
As love.

But how can You love
What I am told is hate?

How can I love
Knowing I disappoint?

How does one heart
Hold so much?

I have gone 'round and 'round
Looking for Truth,

After so long,
I gave up my chase

Because I let myself
Believe there is no hope-

I couldn't trust
That You planned more.

How does one heart
Hold so much?

I let the world
Tell me they knew

All about You -
And maybe they truly do.

But for me that just isn't enough,
I need more.

I want to know Truth,
I want to open that door.

How does one heart
Hold so much?

I am sorry if
I am not enough-

I cannot be
The girl they say to be.

I tried to follow all the rules
And that did not work.

I could still not find You
Or the life You want from me.

How does one heart
Hold so much?

I tried to reject
All that I was -

That got me no further
Than the other paths.

I am ready to give up,

I am ready to quit -

I believe You are there,
But maybe your not.

I just don't know -
Maybe it is better left alone.

How does one heart
Hold so much?

Yet I cannot deny my nature,
As flawed as it is -

I am a seeker, a questioner,
A woman with a mission

And belief
That I can change the world

If only I knew how
To find what You need me to be.

How does one heart
Hold so much?

As much as I try
To push You away,

I can still feel You
Nudging me, trying to say

Something to me
That I cannot hear

Over the loud voices
That tell me You are not here.

How does one heart
Hold so much?

I am learning to battle
The darkness inside.

I am learning to seek You
In ways I did not know.

I am trying to accept,
That the world may have lied.

I am trying,
I am trying.

How does one heart
Hold so much?

You gave me a heart,
You made me this way -

Would you truly feel
That I am a mistake?

I cannot follow rules,
I challenge them all.

I tried to be the good girl,
But every time I fall.

How does one heart
Hold so much?

What do You want?
Do you hate that I doubt?

Or do you love that I question
Just so I can know You?

I believe You are there,
But I do not know

If in the span of forever
If I really matter.

But in this moment
Here and now

I want to believe

You love me.

How does one heart
Hold so much?

I heard your name
And of course I questioned,

But I figured why not?
It cannot be worse.

I whispered the word,
A name so precious

The world hid it.
I whispered Your name.

How does one heart
Hold so much?

As Your name became
More comfortable to my tongue

I thought to try to talk to You
And use that sacred word.

The sweetness of Your name
On my lips as I spoke

Made You feel real
In ways You never were to me.

How does one heart
Hold so much?

So now I feel better,
Because You shared

An intimate part of You
With me.

If You can let Yourself be known,
Why must I hide in shame and fear?

Because I am learning a love
That only You can give me.

How does one heart
Hold so much?

I still hesitate,
I am skeptical and afraid

Of being wrong -
But now I feel that it doesn't matter -

You shared Yourself with me,
You shared Yourself with the world

But they do not all hear You.
They do not all know.

How does one heart
Hold so much?

I don't know if I can do
What You ask of me

But I do know You are there
And pretty sure you love me.

So I will take that love
And do my best

To show it to all your people,
In whatever way that comes to pass.

I will still fail, I will be guilty -
You know my secrets and desires

My heart is not pure as it should be-
But I promise to love anyway.

How does one heart
Hold so much?

How big Your heart must be

To love the world

Filled with hurt and pain
Rejection and injury!

Yet You know each of us
As if each is everything!

I pray for wisdom and strength
To help the whole world know just

How much One heart
Can hold!

My Guide

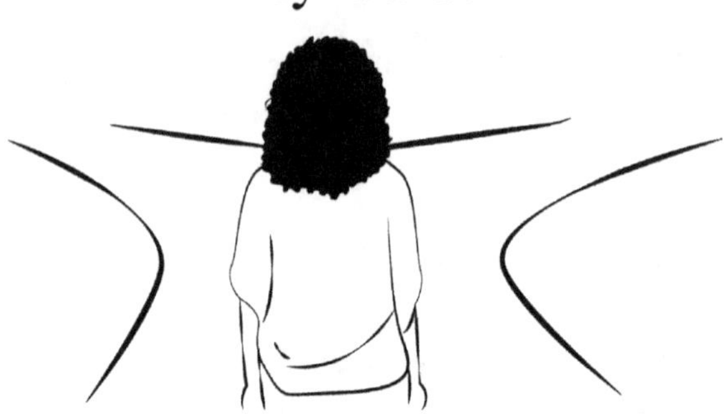

In life's journey,
We have shared a path
Once or twice.

Sometimes I turn
Away
And wander off.

Sometimes I look
And cannot find
Where the road is.

But every time I stray
I turn around
And find

You waiting there,
Welcoming me back
To guide me.

I See

I see You
In the colors
All around me.

I see You
In the sounds
Buzzing in the air.

I see You
In the scents
So sweet to breathe.

I see You
In the softness
Of the petals and clouds.

I see You
In the flavors

Of the world.

I see You
In everyday
All around me.